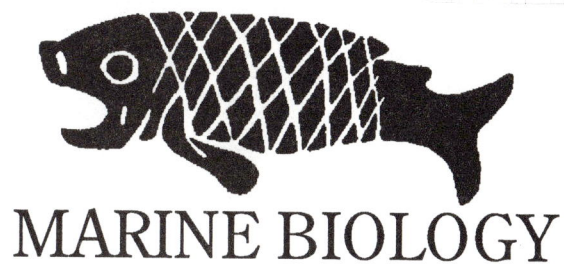

MARINE BIOLOGY

by Joey Tanner

Self-Directed Study Units for Grades K-3 and 4-8, gifted. Easily adaptable for regular classroom use.

Interdisciplinary and Product-Oriented through the use of:

    Evaluating
    Classifying
    Comparing
    Imagining
    Researching
    Mapping & Charting
    Creating
    Reporting
    Thinking . . . Reacting
    Career Exploration

ZEPHYR PRESS
TUCSON, ARIZONA

MARINE BIOLOGY
By Joey Tanner
copyright © 1980
Revised 1992
Zephyr Press
P.O. Box 13448
Tucson, Arizona 85732-3448

ISBN 0-913705-05-5

QH91.16.T36 1992

The purchase of this book entitles the individual teacher to reproduce student copies for use in the classroom. The reproduction of any part for an entire school system or for commercial use is strictly prohibited. No form of this work may be reproduced or transmitted or recorded without written permission from the publisher.

Original Design: Penny Rebholz
Original Illustrations: Martha Payne
Revision Design, Layout and some of the Illustrations: Kathleen Koopman

Educational Consultant: Chris Brewer

CONTENTS

The Premise 4
A Word to the Teacher 5
Rationale for Self-Directed Learning................ 6
    Obstacles to Independent Learning 6
    A Learning Atmosphere 6
From Passive Learner to Active Participant 8
The Format 9
Suggested Readings............................... 10
Interest Development Center 11
Getting Started 12

MARINE BIOLOGY
    Unit I: Kindergarten Through Third Grade....... 15
    Unit II: Grades Four Through Eight............ 29
    Key to Words from the Sea 50
Bibliography 51
Exploring the Arts 53

THE PREMISE
Learning Is Natural

Children are active participants in their learning,
*   not passive vessels to be filled.*

They are always seeking and choosing
*   what they will learn and what they*
*   will not learn.*

Their interest, trust and active
*   involvement is crucial.*

Children tend to become personally
*   involved in projects that appeal to a*
*   variety of modalities . . .*
* reading, writing, reasoning, building,*
*   imagining, and creating.*

What a gift we give when we respect the
*   child's natural need to explore, to*
*   reflect, to communicate, to dream,*
*   to celebrate!*

Available as a poster from Zephyr Press.

A WORD TO THE TEACHER

Marine Biology

From the smallest plankton to the most massive whales, marine biology is the study of the flora and fauna, the living creatures of the ocean.

The study of marine biology includes the delicate inter-relationships between the organisms that make up the complex patterns of the food chains, the ecology of the sea. The sea remains a major source of food. As the earth becomes more and more populated, conserving the life support system of the sea becomes a serious concern.

Careers in marine biology and related fields are fascinating to many young people today. Much of the sea still remains a mystery, but new instruments for drilling and dredging the ocean floor make the sea one of the world's remaining frontiers.

RATIONALE FOR SELF-DIRECTED LEARNING

Our children's education must be more than the memorization of capitals of the states, the products of the countries, and dates and places of past wars. Most teachers and parents would agree that what is also wanted is for our children to learn to think for themselves, to organize their own time, to make wise choices, to work independently, and to thoughtfully evaluate the results of their study.

Obstacles to Independent Learning

In spite of the teacher's best efforts, many, if not most, classroom settings are organized in such a way that students are involved in schedules and organizational plans that foster dependence rather than the independence we prefer. Students are told what is to be learned and how long it will take them to learn it. The teacher not only defines the resources, but also decides whether the learning experience was a satisfactory and valuable one.

"One can learn the campaigns of the Civil War with dates, battles, and characters without learning anything about why wars are fought between friends or what ideas can be generalized to other conflict situations."

—James Gallagher,
Teaching the Gifted Child, 1985

A Learning Atmosphere

Each time we, as educators, focus on what our objectives are, we need to take a fresh look at our classroom mode of operation and evaluate the effectiveness of the way we teach. Quite naturally, for most of us, our teaching style has had more to do with how we were taught than with what recent research has shown about the learning process. Even our good instincts have been overcome by the years of conditioning we have known in our own educational process.

Like a breath of fresh air, the recent findings coming from the research on the brain and how it operates are supporting intuitive knowledge. This research is showing that our brains are receptive to learning only under certain conditions. Our job is to translate that information into a classroom atmosphere that provides

- challenge
- freedom within structure
- trust and warmth
- opportunities to experience success
- personal involvement in the curriculum

A natural transition generally occurs that transforms the former "teacher-lecturer" into a "fellow-learner." As a "fellow-learner," the teacher becomes a resource person, a facilitator, a classroom manager. In this maturing atmosphere, students gradually come to see themselves as responsible for their own learning, and a foundation for self-direction is set.

At this point, a sometimes unexpected problem arises. We find students no more ready for their independent learning than we, as teachers, are ready to allow it. The common occurrence is mentioned repeatedly in the literature dealing with programming for the gifted, an area in which independent study and research are recommended as major curricular activities. See the Suggested Reading List: Maker (1982), Doherty and Evans (1980), and Feldhusen and Treffinger (1980).

FROM PASSIVE LEARNER TO ACTIVE PARTICIPANT
(Bridging the Gap)

The Zephyr self-directed study unit was developed expressly to bridge that gap: to transport the student from the position of passive recipient to that of an active participant in his/her own pursuit of knowledge.

Within the defined structure of each unit, the students are given opportunities to
- make choices
- learn at their own pace
- learn in a manner more closely suited to their own learning style
- expand their research skills
- use a variety of modalities
- plan their own time
- develop the skills of creative, critical, and evaluative thinking
- experience whole-brain learning

As assuming responsibility for directing their own learning is so often an unfamiliar situation, the students will need your encouragement at the start. Generally, within six to nine weeks, most students will be well on their way from teacher-dependence to self-motivation. (Beginning the venture with only a few choices, then gradually arranging the setting so that there are more and more choices works best.) As students assume more responsibility, many teachers begin to consider the school library as just another part of the classroom. The benefits are many, from gaining a personal relationship with the librarian to learning about the enormous resources available in most school libraries.

Eventually, a few students will be ready for a true investigative research study of professional quality as suggested by Joseph Renzulli in the *Enrichment Triad Model: A Guide for Developing Defensible Programs for the Gifted and Talented*, 1977.

THE FORMAT

Originally developed for gifted students, these units emphasize the use of higher-level thinking skills and are appropriate for use in any classroom where the goal is to encourage students to become responsible for their own education.

Interdisciplinary in content, the unit envelops a broad view of the topic by integrating the "basics" into each activity.

Within this book are two complete units: one created for the lower elementary gifted student and one for the upper elementary gifted student. Suggestions for adapting or adjusting either of the levels to fit any individual classroom are included.

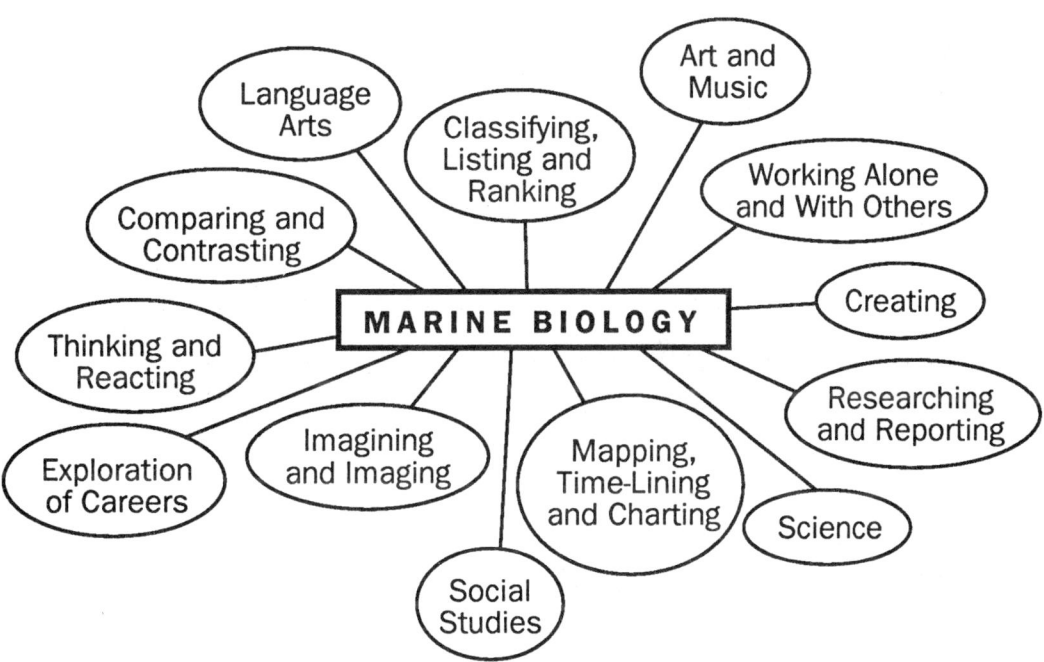

SUGGESTED READINGS
Self-directed Study

Barbe, W. and J. Renzulli. *Psychology and Education of the Gifted.* New York: Irvington Publications, 1982.

Brewer, Chris and Don G. Campbell. *Rhythms of Learning: Creative Tools for Developing Lifelong Skills.* Tucson, Ariz.: Zephyr Press, 1991.

Clark, B. *Growing Up Gifted.* Columbus, Ohio: Merrill Publishing Company, 1988.

Feldhusen and Treffinger. *Creative Thinking and Problem Solving in Gifted Education.* Dubuque, Iowa: Kendall-Hunt Publishing, 1980.

Maker, C.J. *Curriculum Development for the Gifted.* Rockville, Md.: Aspens Systems Corporation, 1982.

Malehorn, H. *Open to Change: Options for Teaching Self-Directed Learners.* Palo Alto, Calif.: Scott Foresman Company, 1978.

Purkey, W.W. *Inviting School Success, A Self Concept Approach to Teaching and Learning.* Belmont, Calif.: Wadsworth Publishing Company, Inc., 1978.

Renzulli, J. *Enrichment Triad Model: A Guide for Developing Defensible Programs for the Gifted and Talented.* Mansfield, Conn.: Creative Learning Press, 1977.

Udall, Anne J. and Joan E. Daniels. *Creating the Thoughtful Classroom: Strategies to Promote Student Thinking.* Tucson, Ariz.: Zephyr Press, 1991.

INTEREST DEVELOPMENT CENTER
Marine Biology

The purpose of this interest center is to stimulate interest in the topic area. Students need time for browsing and investigating for maximum benefit. These are beginning ideas... you and your students will think of more... let parents and other teachers know more about the center, and it will grow many times without effort.

Books and posters
Sea life
Sailing myths
Tropical fish
Jacques Cousteau
Aquarium building
Shell identification
Sea exploration
Ecology of the sea
Songs of the sea
Mermaids
Fishing guides
> Be sure to include books above grade level.

Art Supplies
Water colors, chalk, oil pastels, polyform, clay, markers, and various textures of paper.

Objects and artifacts
Shells and coral
Large box or container of sand
Fishing gear and net
An anchor
Whale bones
Compass
An aquarium
Magnifying glass
Canned foods, products of the sea

Videos, Filmstrips, Loops and Slides
Maps
Globes
Magazines, especially copies of *National Geographic,* oceans, sea magazines, and marine mammals (and other ocean-oriented magazines.)

Songs and Sounds of the Sea
Paul Winter: "Callings, Celebration of the Voices of the Sea"
David Blonski: "Dance of the Dolphin"
Claude Debussy "Nocturnes from Serenes" and "La Mer"
"Pachelbel Music for Meditation" (Canon in D with ocean)
"Bach for Relaxation" (Air from the Suite in D Major)
Anton Rubenstein: "The Ocean"

GETTING STARTED

1. Select a topic as an extension of a regular subject (particularly when your class seems to crave more), or select a topic to pursue that is of particular interest and may not be a part of the curriculum. To zero in on special interests, administer an interest survey to each student.

2. Copy the unit for each student. When using these units for the entire class, you may want to expand or delete activities for individual students.

3. Set up a center in the classroom that encourages exploration in the subject field. You'll want to include a wide variety of materials. Be creative—the purpose of the center is to excite the students, so begin with lots of "hands on" materials. Allow for ample browsing time and encourage students to investigate and become absorbed.

4. Go over each activity in the unit with the students, discussing and answering any questions. You as Teacher are the key to successful implementation. Because most children are already well versed in the "One Right Answer Game," they will need encouragement to branch out into many of the open-ended activities in the packets.

5. Set the stage. Plan to conference as needed; provide resources as needed. Then, get out of the way and let your students learn.

6. Give as much time as each student needs to complete each activity in the unit. The entire packet might take from five to ten weeks or longer.

7. As each activity is completed and evaluated, initial the activity near each number. You will want to evaluate on the basis of the response that is appropriate for each individual student.

8. When a student shows extreme interest in the topic, the completion of this unit might be only the beginning. This student may be ready for further study and research and needs only the resources, guidance, and freedom to pursue his/her well-planned project.

To prepare for further research, students will need to decide:

- What will the study be; what will be investigated and produced?
- Where will the background information be found (i.e., speakers, interviews, books, films, microfiche, documents)?
- What, exactly, will be the form of the product: a model, a manuscript, or?
- Who might be interested in the product: professionals in the field, publishers, organizations . . . ?
- What is needed to begin: specific plans, resources, deadlines . . . ?

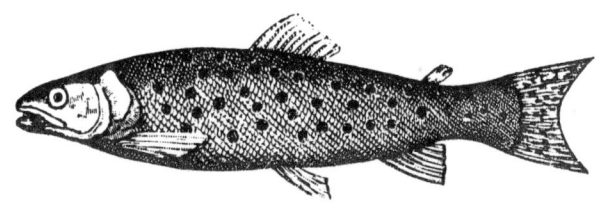

Suggestions for Adapting the Unit to Your Particular Learning Situation

- Require fewer, or more, research sources.

- Assign more of the activities to small groups instead of to individual students.

- Give fewer or more choices.

- Delete some activities altogether.

- Arrange the unit to be a class project with students choosing different parts to complete.

- Add some activities of your own.

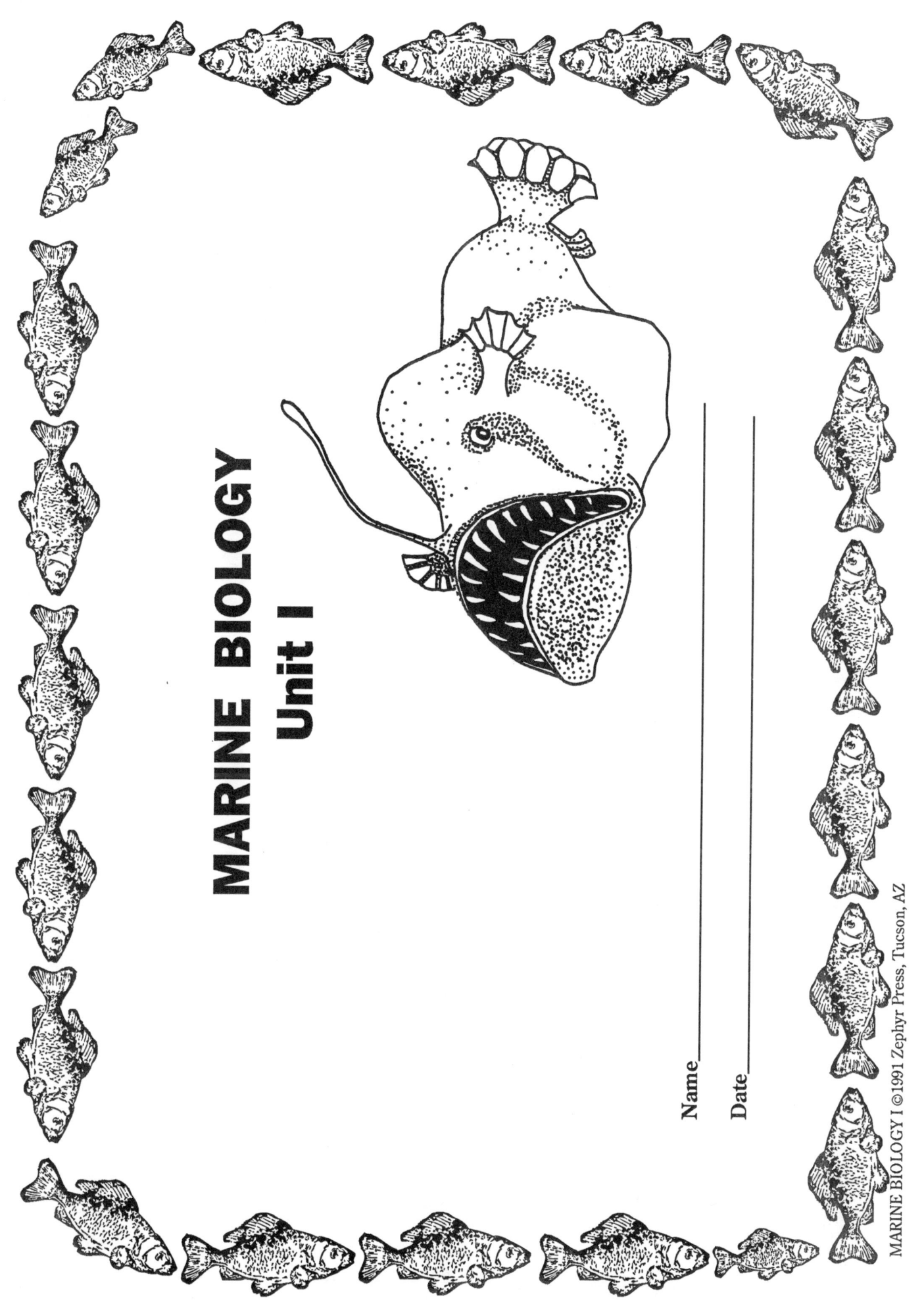

MARINE BIOLOGY
Unit I

Name _____

Date _____

1 SETTING THE STAGE

Have you visited the ocean?

Have you tasted the salty water and breathed in the special smell of the sea?

Have you dug into the wet sand and found the curious creatures there?

Have you seen and felt the shells on the seashore?

Listen to some ocean music . . .

Close your eyes and imagine you are there . . . feel the moist air on your skin . . . (is it warm or cool?) . . . breath in the air . . . let everything you want to see come to your mind . . . notice the colors . . . the smells . . . the sounds . . .

DESCRIBE your experience without using words. Instead, use gestures and music mimicking the sounds of the ocean.

PERFORM your pantomime in front of friends using a background of color. Invite others to share their nonverbal experiences. Remember to include feelings in your interpretations.

MARINE BIOLOGY I ©1991 Zephyr Press, Tucson, AZ

2 GO . . . TO THE LIBRARY!

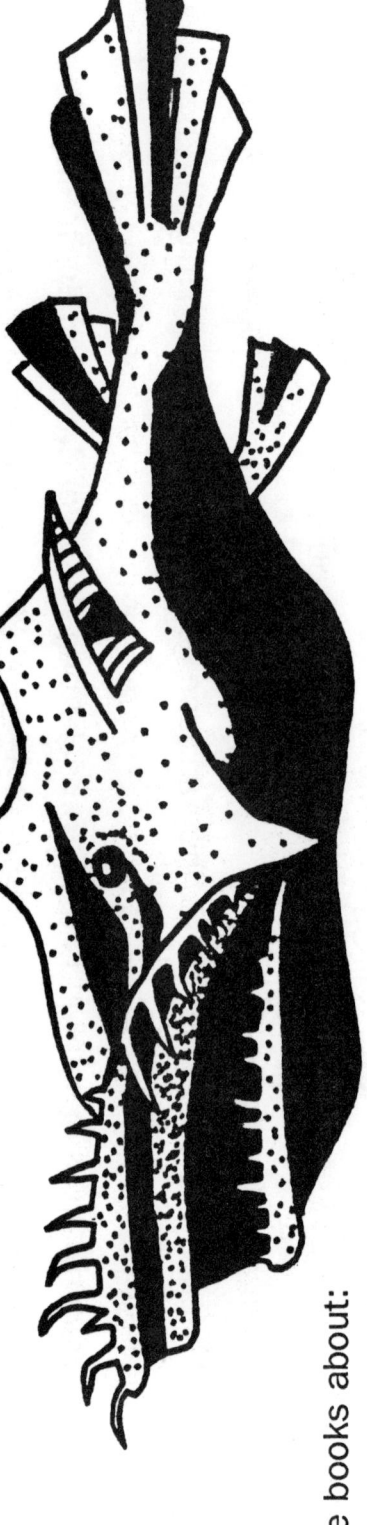

FIND some books about:
- whales and dolphins
- the ocean
- shells
- saltwater fish
- anything else about sea life

NOTICE especially:
- the parts of the sea . . . the reef . . . the abyss
- where different kinds of sealife live
- the sedentary feeders
- poisonous sea animals
- whales and dolphins
- sea shells
- the food chain of the sea
- the life cycle of the salmon

3 FIND OUT

FIND OUT about:
- the manatee
- the coelacanth
- plankton
- sea anemone
- tropical fish
- starfish
- the octopus
- jellyfish

WHAT do these creatures have in common?
WHERE might they fit in the food chain?

Listen to "Pachelbel Music for Meditation" (Canon in D with Ocean) or "Bach for Relaxation" (Air from the Suite in D Major).

Cover a sheet of drawing paper with many bright colors of crayons . . . color it solid. Then cover the bright colors with black . . . solid.

Now scratch an underwater scene of some of these marine animals.

(See if you can find the painting "Fish Magic" by Paul Klee.)

MARINE BIOLOGY I ©1991 Zephyr Press, Tucson, AZ

4 RESEARCH AND REPORT (Choose one)

FIND OUT about poisonous sea animals. Make a chart showing what some look like. Label each one.

FIND OUT about at least two kinds of whales. Listen to the sounds and songs of the whale while you make models of them. Label each one.

FIND OUT about sea shells. Put together a collection of shells. (Ask your friends to help you find them.) Label each one.

PUT TOGETHER a display in your classroom or in the library.

Include: Books
           Artwork
           Videos

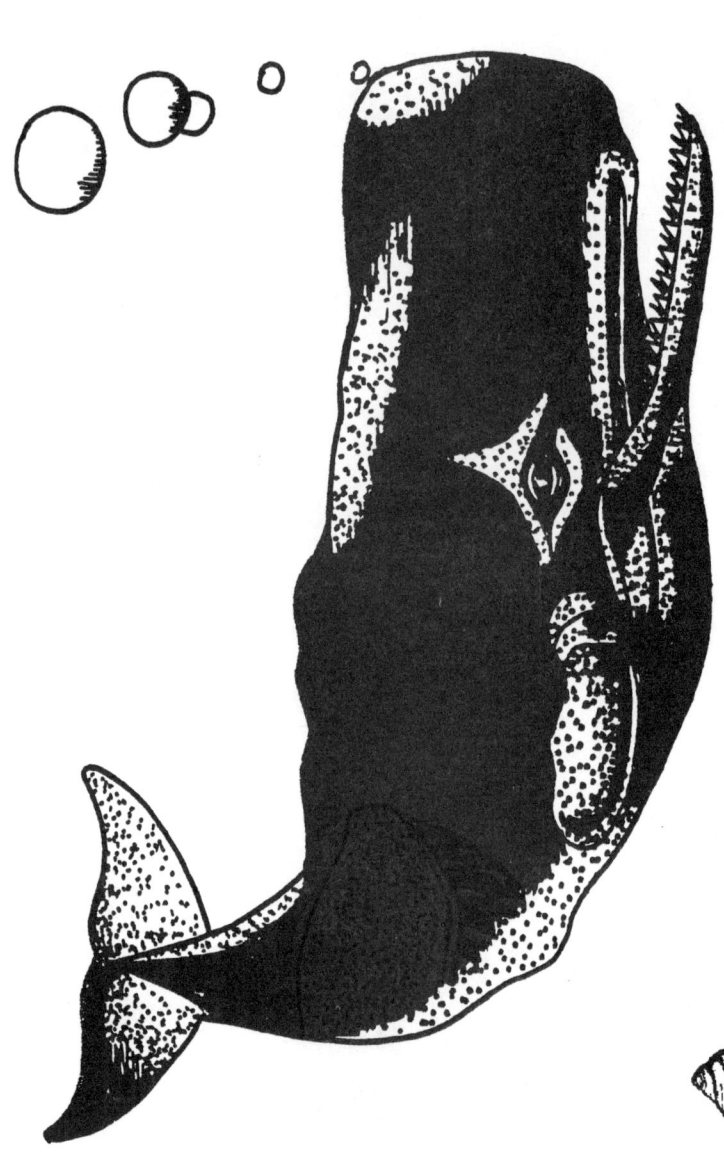

MARINE BIOLOGY I ©1991 Zephyr Press, Tucson, AZ

5 ENDANGERED SPECIES

Write a letter to—
Greenpeace U.S.A.
1436 U St., N.W.
Washington, D.C. 20009

Tell them you want to know which sea animals might become extinct.

DECIDE which endangered sea animals should be saved. Make a mobile showing them.

OR

FIND OUT about prehistoric sea creatures, such as the mosasaurus, and the elasosaurus.

In what period did they live?
How big were they?
Where did they live?
Where were the remains found?
What did they eat?
Why did they become extinct?

MAKE a model of one of these prehistoric sea creatures using modeling clay. Place it in your box of sand.

MARINE BIOLOGY I ©1991 Zephyr Press, Tucson, AZ

CREATIVE WRITING

Pretend you are a deep sea diver. You are going into a part of the sea unknown to man.

Are you afraid? . . . excited? . . . What do you feel? Tell the story of what happened by making a tape (with sound effects)

OR

by writing a story.
(You can bind it into a book with your own illustrations.)

7 BY YOURSELF

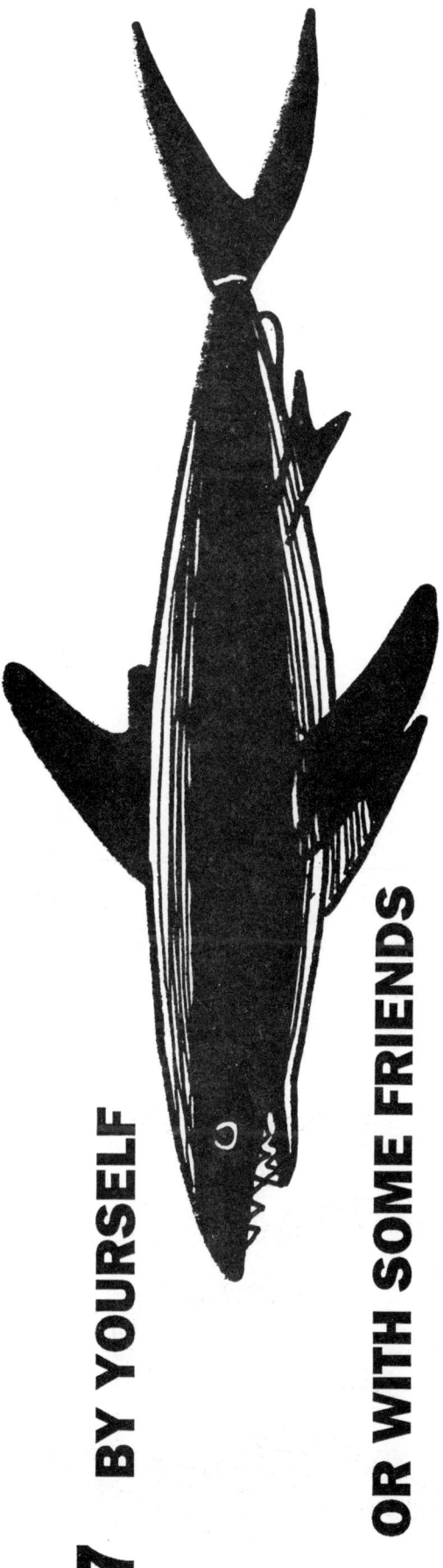

OR WITH SOME FRIENDS

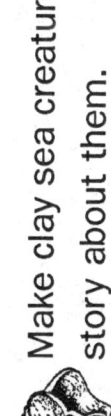 Make a mural showing the "marine biome." Show some of the sea life in each region.

OR

Make clay sea creatures (real or imaginary). Place them in your box of sand. Now tell a story about them.

OR

Fill a large plastic basin with water. Gently rock it back and forth and watch the movement of the water make waves. Listen to ocean sounds and explore ways to move like a wave.

MARINE BIOLOGY I ©1991 Zephyr Press, Tucson, AZ

8 FIND OUT ABOUT MARINE BIOLOGY

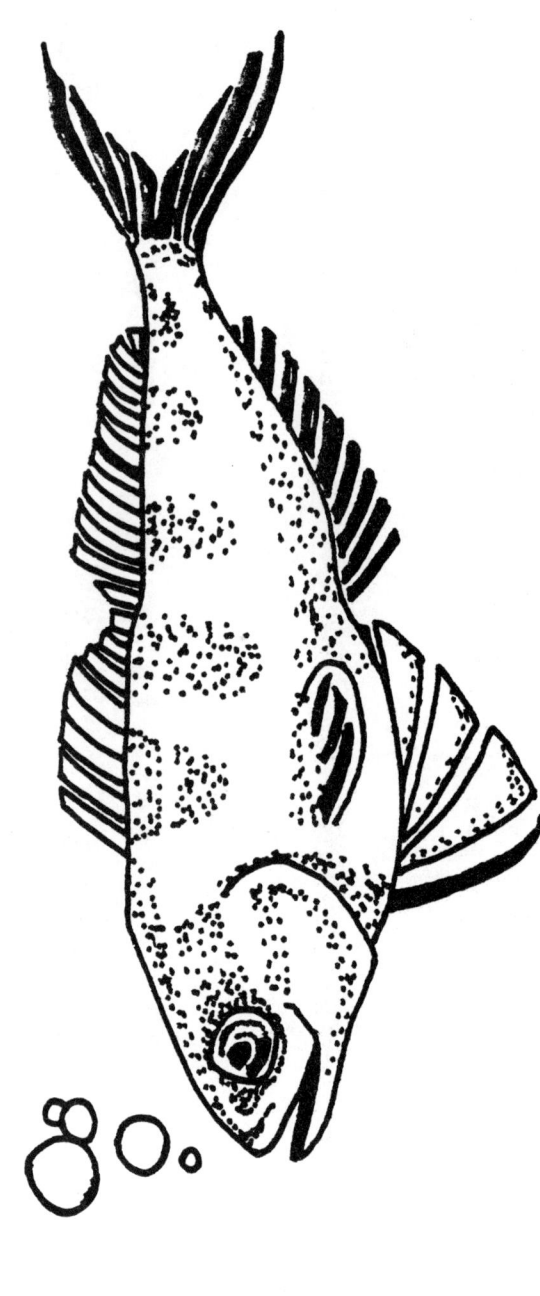

- Invite a marine biologist to talk to your class.
  What education and training do you need to become a marine biologist?
  Ask the marine biologist what his or her reasons were for becoming a marine biologist.

OR

- Plan for your class to see a video about Jacques Cousteau.
  What does a marine biologist do that you would enjoy?
  What does a marine biologist do that you would not enjoy?

9 LEGENDS AND STORIES

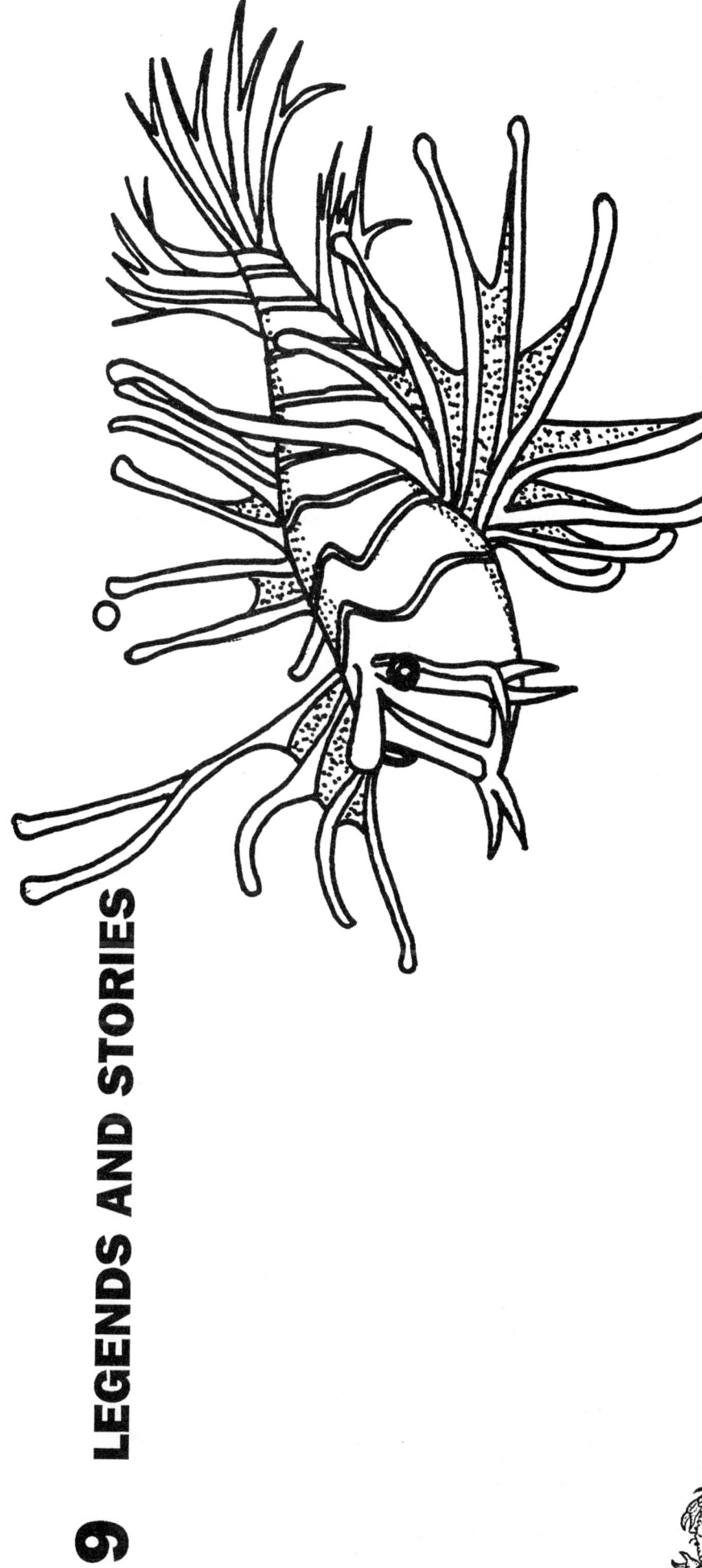

WATCH some videos or have someone read some stories to you about:

- mermaids
- sea nymphs

OR

WHAT purpose did legends serve the people who sailed the sea? Why was it important? Find out about other legendary characters such as Neptune or Poseidon. What is their relation to other Greek or Roman legendary characters?

Create a song or poem about mermaids or sea nymphs.

MARINE BIOLOGY I ©1991 Zephyr Press, Tucson, AZ

10 ISLANDS AND SEACOASTS

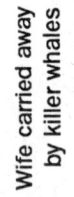

EXPLORE the lives of people who live on islands and seacoasts:

Pacific NW Indian tribes

Irish sea-going communities

Norwegian people

South Seas islanders

Japanese fishermen

How do people of different cultures use and depend on the marine environment for food, clothing and jewelry, transportation or tools?

Show your class what you have learned.

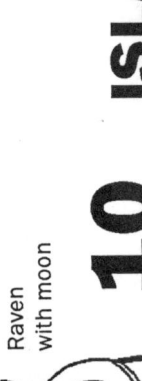
Raven with moon

Frog

Salmon in lake

Raven

Beaver

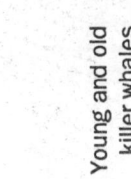
Dogfish

Wife carried away by killer whales

Young and old killer whales

MARINE BIOLOGY I ©1991 Zephyr Press, Tucson, AZ

11 MAN AND DOLPHIN

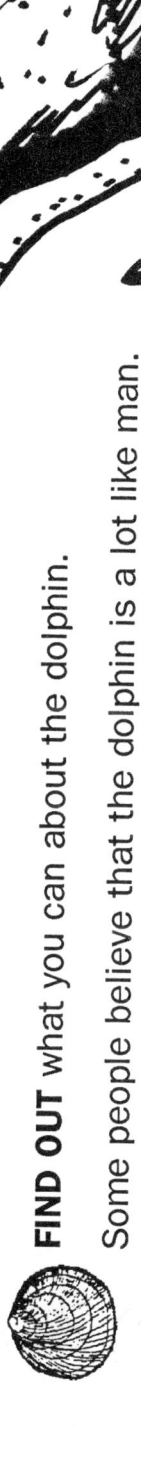

FIND OUT what you can about the dolphin.

Some people believe that the dolphin is a lot like man.

How are we alike?

How are we different?

Why do you think we are so similar?

(Be sure you find out about their family life.)

12 WORDS FROM THE SEA

DOWN

1. Dangerous to man
2. A sea animal with a hard shell and claws.

ACROSS

3. Very intelligent sea animal.
4. A region of the ocean filled with coral.
5. A fish that swims upstream to mate and die.

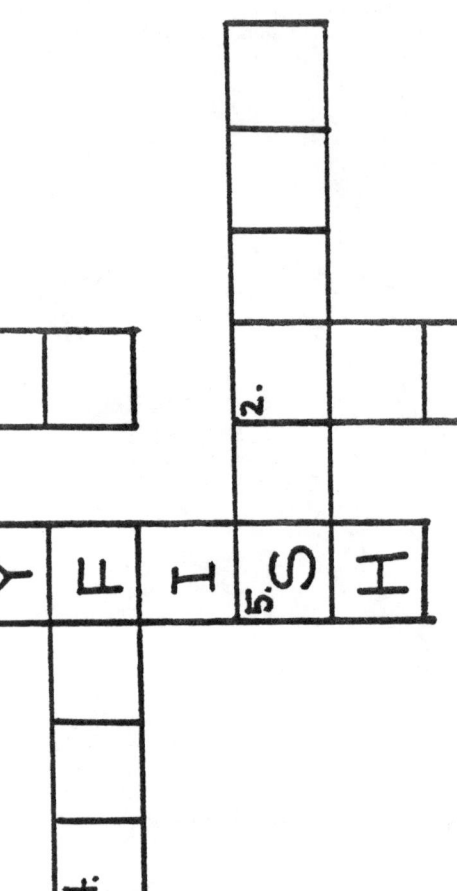

MARINE BIOLOGY I ©1991 Zephyr Press, Tucson, AZ

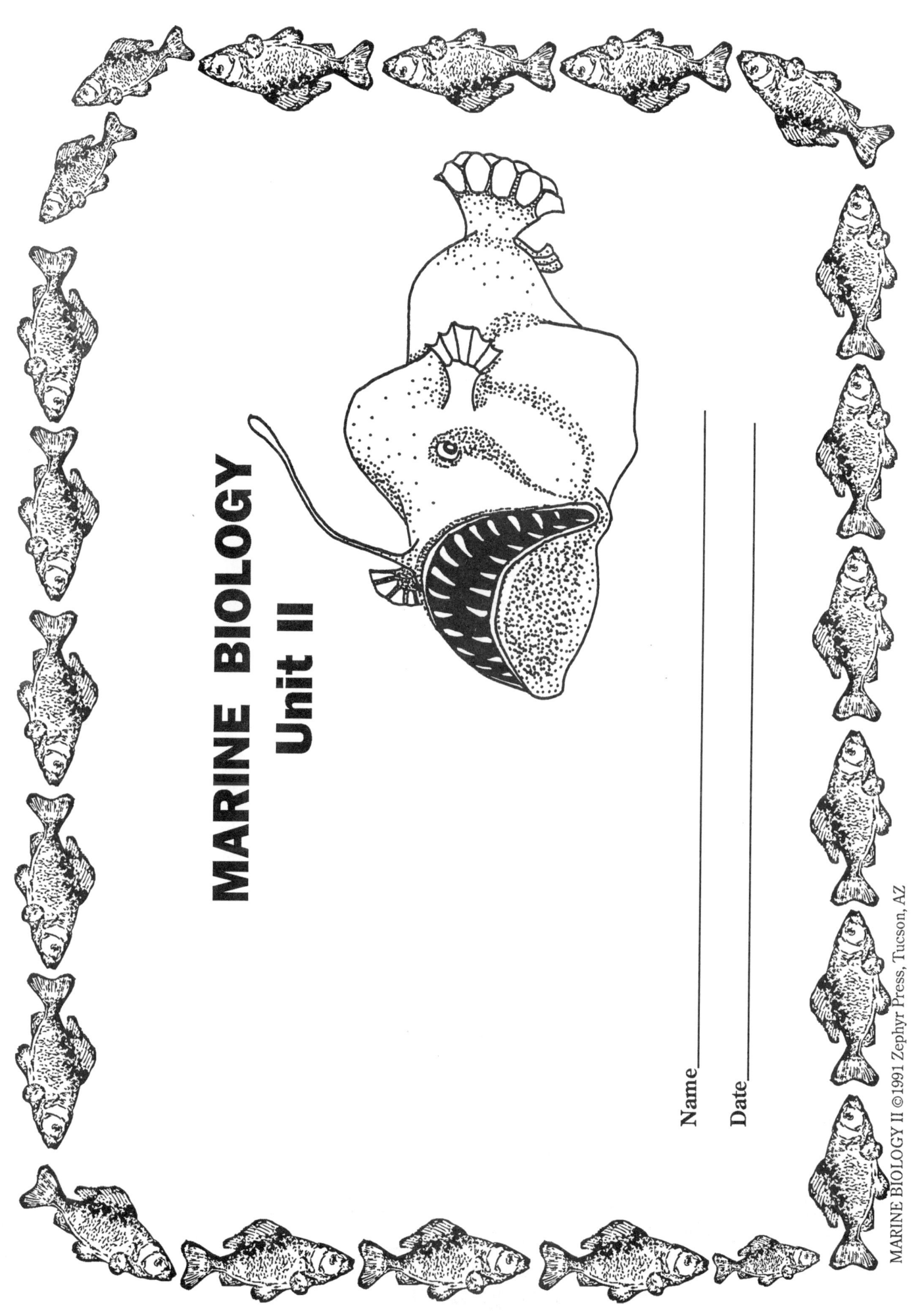

1 SETTING THE STAGE

"The ocean ... offers us an incessant and infinite display of its most marvelous treasures. There was a continuous change of decor and scenery, as if staged to please our vision, and we were called upon not only to contemplate the works of the creator in this spanse of liquid world, but also to delve into the most redoubtable mysteries of the sea."

Jules Verne

Twenty Thousand Leagues Under the Sea

Take some time for quiet ... listen to "The Ocean" by Anton Rubenstein ... "La Mer" by Claude Debussy ... some sea chanteys ... and any other music that might set the mood for a study of the sea and its life ...

Draw or paint a picture that reflects your experiences as you listen to the music. Think about the quote by Jules Verne. Imagine yourself being there ... include imaginings of the sounds, the smells, the colors, the shapes ...

2 GO . . . TO THE LIBRARY

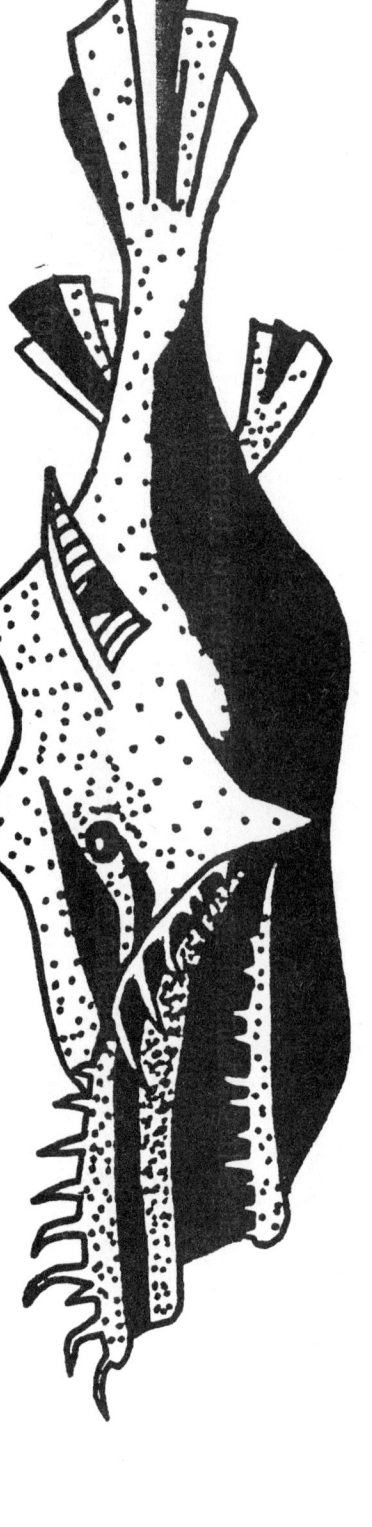

COLLECT as many "mermaid" stories as you can. Be sure to include Hans Christian Anderson's *Little Mermaid* and Jean Girdoux's *Ondine*. Listen to "Nocturnes from Serenes" by Claude Debussy.

OR

FIND the answers to these legendary facts:

- Why does the mermaid look into a mirror?
- Why is there salt in the sea?
- In the Fiji Islands, what do they give as the reason for the fowl crowing?
- How did the coconut come to be created?
- Why do fish open and close their mouths?
- Why does the jellyfish have no shell?
- Why is the water warm below the surface of the sea?

THEN CREATE a way to communicate your feelings (video, tape recordings, a series of one-act plays or write your own legendary story about mermaids). Present your product to a group of your choice.

MARINE BIOLOGY II ©1991 Zephyr Press, Tucson, AZ

3 RESEARCH AND REPORT

Listen to the sounds and songs of whales.

EXPLORE the problem of the balance of nature as it applies to sea life.

OR

INVESTIGATE products used by man that originate in the whale. What part of the whale is used for each product? How has the future of the whale been affected by humans? What products used by man are made from sea plants? What is found in sea plants that is so valuable? What particular plants are used for these purposes?

OR

RESEARCH the many areas of the sea—the reef, the abyss . . . become familiar with the sea life found in each.

THEN REPORT on the topic in the way of your choice

☐ A magazine type article
☐ A video
☐ A tape recording

MARINE BIOLOGY II ©1991 Zephyr Press, Tucson, AZ

4 CLASSIFY—LIST—RANK

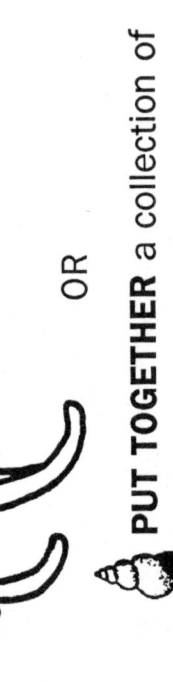

RESEARCH symbolic relationships observed in the sea. Separate your feelings into "communalism" and "parasitism" symbols.

OR

FIND OUT about sedentary feeders. Make a chart diagramming their environment. Be sure to distinguish and label their different methods of collecting food.

OR

RESEARCH poisonous sea life. Rank, illustrate and label them according to the degree of venom and their danger to man.

OR

PUT TOGETHER a collection of at least twelve varieties of shells. Classify and label each one.
THEN Find some books, videos and illustrations on your subject and set up a display in the library.

OR

SELECT 3 to 5 common varieties of the whale. Make a model of each one . . . classify and label them. Put them in your box of sand.

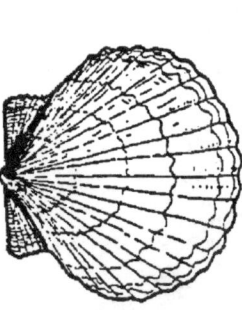

MARINE BIOLOGY II ©1991 Zephyr Press, Tucson, AZ

5 ENDANGERED SPECIES

INFORM yourself about endangered species of the sea by writing to—

Greenpeace U.S.A.
1436 U St., N.W.
Washington, D.C. 20009

Decide which animal you are most concerned about.

- ☐ Write a news article
- ☐ Write a TV of radio commentary
- ☐ Put together a poster
- ☐ _____
  (Your idea)

Present your product to someone who might use it to inform others.

FIND OUT (choose two)

 **WHICH** sea animals can break the pressure barriers?

 **WHAT** are some superstitions that are inspired by the sea urchins?

 **HOW** might the dolphin be used in naval intelligence?

 **WHAT** is the curious story of the tilefish?

 **WHAT** is the purpose of the International Whaling Commission?

 **WHAT** is the meaning of "Predators follow predators that follow predators."?

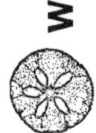 **WHAT** is the relationship of the crown-of-thorns to the coral reef?

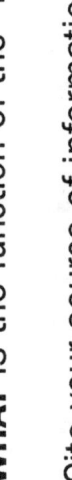 **WHAT** is the function of the "lateral line" organ?

Cite your source of information.

CREATIVE WRITING

WRITE an imaginary story, poem or song based on factual information, using one of these topics. (If you have one you like better, use it!)

- The rule of marine life—to survive and to perpetuate his kind.
- The ritual of the Caribbean spiny lobster.
- The family life of the seal.
- The salmon and its life cycle.
- Unusual behavior patterns of marine life.

8 MAPPING...TIME LINES

DRAW a map of the earth showing spawning grounds (label kinds of fish and type of eggs produced) or migration paths of sea life.

OR

RESEARCH the history of the study of marine biology. How has marine biology changed over time?

What do you attribute these changes to?

What impact has technology had on the field of marine biology?

THEN PREPARE a time line showing the significant events beginning with the first century A.D.

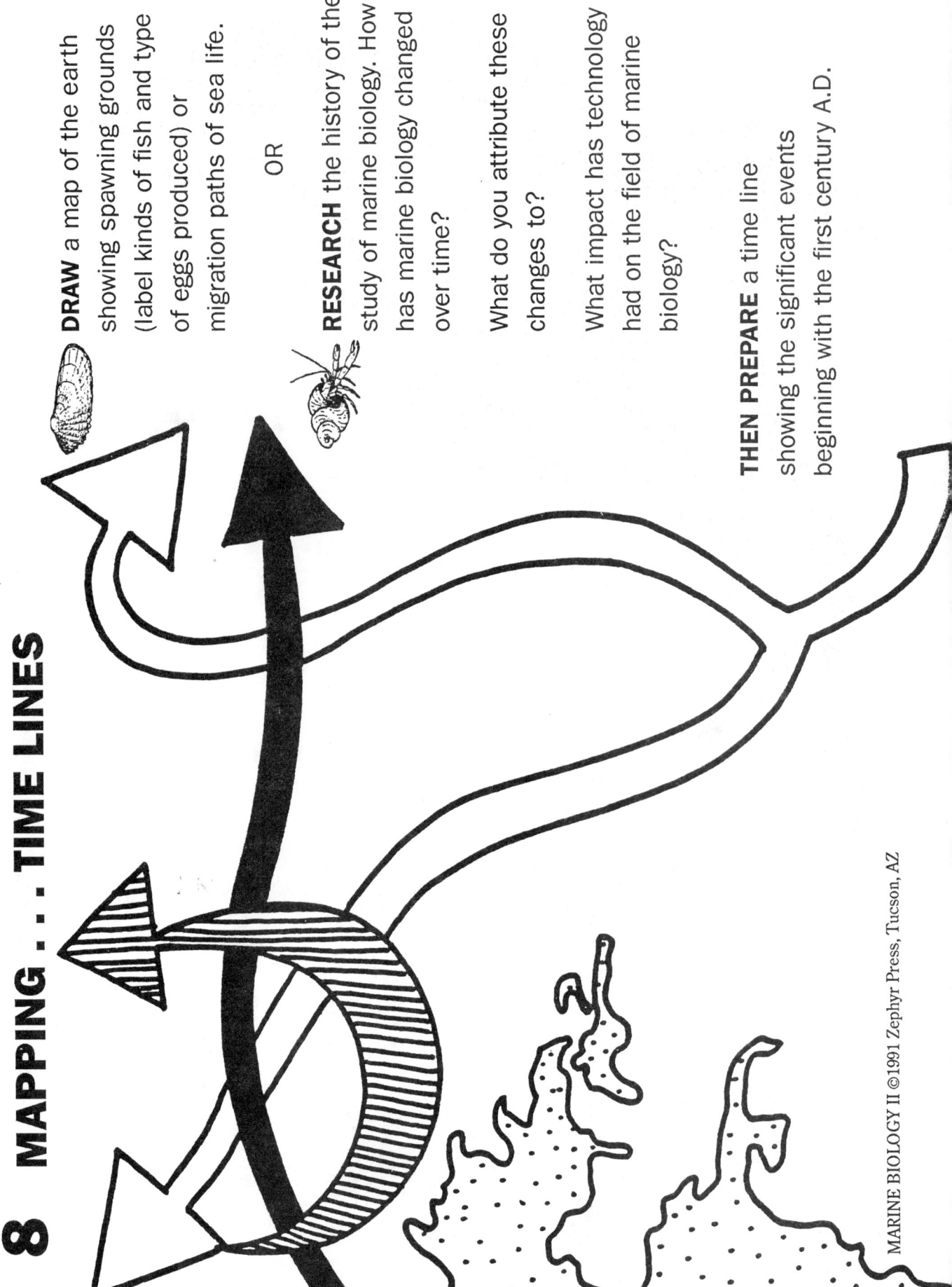

9 MAN AND DOLPHIN

COMPARE and **CONTRAST** the lives of man and the dolphin.
How are we alike and how are we different?

Be sure to include:

- Gestation time
- Length of parental protection
- Age when weaned
- Age of sexual maturity
- Communication
- Senses
- Needs for own territory
- Family ties
- Purpose in life

SHARE YOUR FINDINGS in a way that you choose.

MARINE BIOLOGY II ©1991 Zephyr Press, Tucson, AZ

10 FIND OUT ABOUT

CONSULT newspaper articles to find out answers to the following questions.

What are some possible effects of feeding dolphins in their natural environment?

Of these effects, decide which is the most important. Why is that most important?

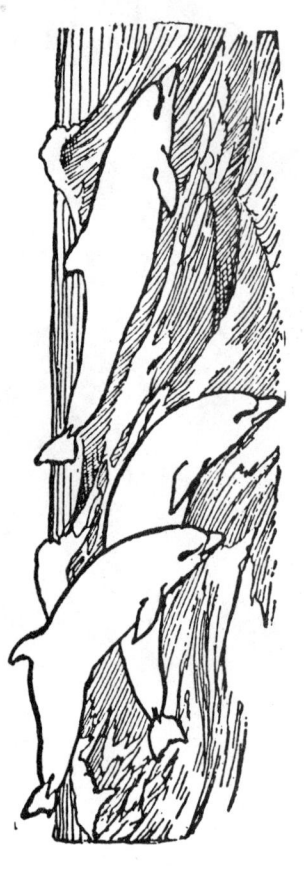

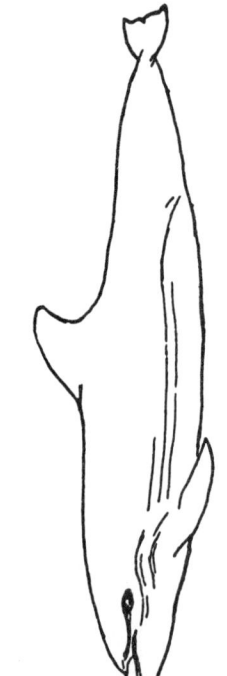

For the following general statement, explain why you agree or disagree with it.

"We, as humans, have the right to interfere with the natural lives of marine animals."

EXPLAIN your reasoning.

MARINE BIOLOGY II ©1991 Zephyr Press, Tucson, AZ

11 BY YOURSELF

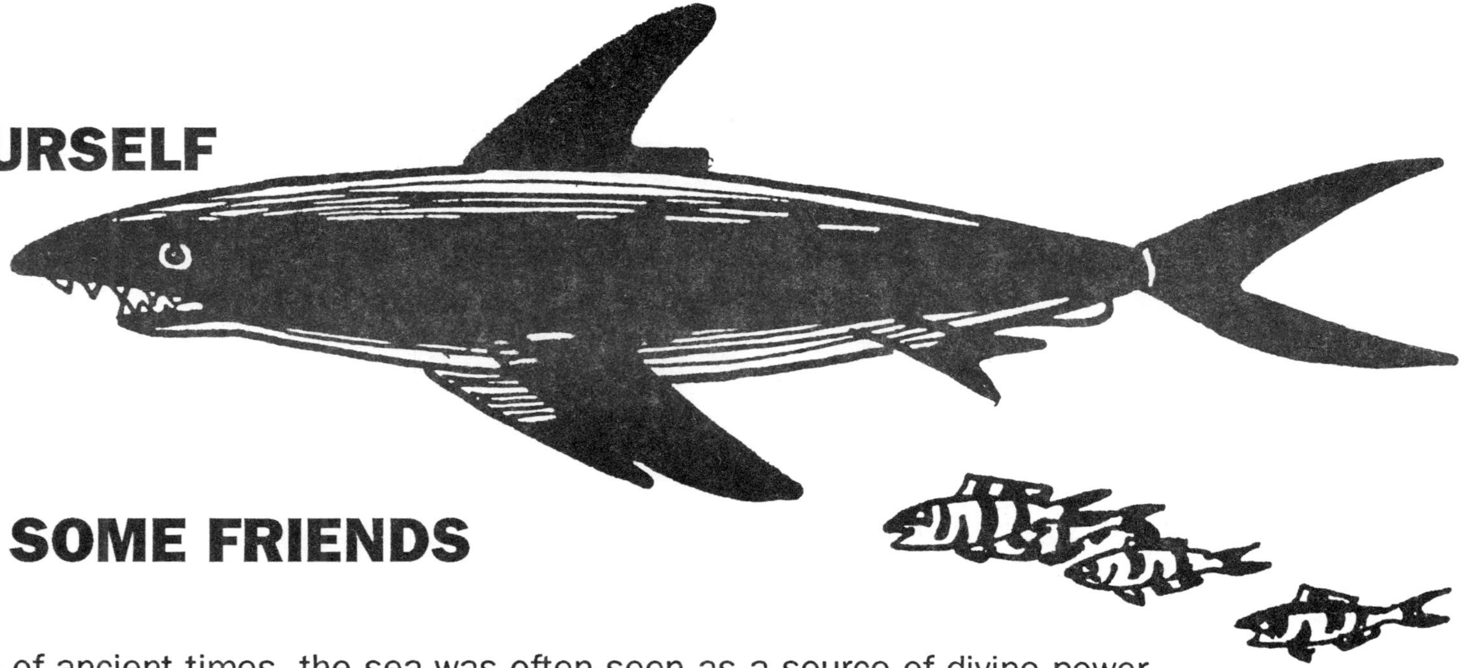

OR WITH SOME FRIENDS

In the myths and stories of ancient times, the sea was often seen as a source of divine power.

Find references (at several points in history, if possible) about some of the following:

- The mermaids
- The sea nymph
- The Poseidon
- Sedna
- The dolphin
- The whale

 **WRITE** and present a play using one or more of these characters.

12 COMPARE AND CONTRAST

CHOOSE ONE

 **DISCOVER** what is alike and what is different about the "true" and the "soft" coral. AND what are the stages of growth of a coral colony from the original parent . . . to the coral skeleton.

  **COMPARE** and **contrast** the salmon and lamprey.

TRACE the fish as it appears in myths and religion. Select several of these and consider what is alike and what is different.

 **COMPARE** and **contrast** the Earth and Mars as they relate to the availability of water. Speculate about the possibility of marine like of Mars.

 **CONSIDER** the similiarity of salt content in human blood and sea water. What conclusions have been drawn from this?

 **COMPARE** the methods of the jellyfish and the anemone for securing "prey."

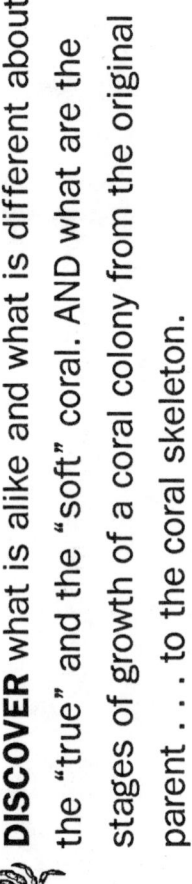

MARINE BIOLOGY II ©1991 Zephyr Press, Tucson, AZ

13 THE FUTURE

RESEARCH man's future as it relates to the sea. How will the sea be of value to man? Write a scholarly presentation of your views in light of the scientific studies so far. Cite at least three sources.

IMAGINE that due to overpopulation, there isn't enough room for people on land. CREATE an undersea colony. DRAW a picture of what it would look like. DESCRIBE how it works. How might you make this undersea colony self-sufficient? How might you keep the water from coming in?

CHOOSE ONE

AND THE PAST

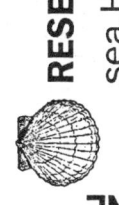

IMAGINE it is 3 billion years ago. Write your story, draw a picture, or create a clay scene of your version of the beginning of life on this planet.

INCLUDE your thoughts about whether it was an accident or whether there is a plan and purpose to life . . . or both.

WRITE a convincing argument for your ideas . . . cite at least 3 sources that may or may not concur with what you believe to be true.

MARINE BIOLOGY II ©1991 Zephyr Press, Tucson, AZ

14 SEACOAST AND ISLAND CULTURES

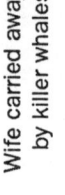

Dogfish

Wife carried away by killer whales

Young and old killer whales

EXPLORE the lives of people who live on islands and seacoasts:

- ✓ Pacific NW Indian tribes
- ✓ Irish sea-going communities
- ✓ Norwegian people
- ✓ South Seas islanders
- ✓ Japanese fisherman

THEN COMPARE how people of different cultures use and depend on the marine environment for food, clothing and jewelry, transportation or tools.

How do the lives of people affect the marine environment?
How can we protect and live in harmony with the marine environment?

WRITE a song or create a rap with your friends about humans and the marine environment.

Raven with moon

Frog

Salmon in lake

Raven

Beaver

MARINE BIOLOGY II ©1991 Zephyr Press, Tucson, AZ

15 MORE...

FIND some pictures that show how different seacoast and island cultures include ocean creatures in their art work.

- Make a list or draw pictures of the different ways a fish can be used by people.

    OR

- Find pictures of Japanese fish prints or make your own by covering a real fish from the market with paint or ink. Lay a sheet of paper on top of the fish and 'pull' a print.

    OR

- Create something for your own use out of a shell.

    OR

- Make clay models of the different types of boats ocean-going cultures have used for transportation.

16 IMAGINE THIS

Another oil spill has ocurred off the coast of Malibu, California.

FIND OUT more about this imaginary major oil spill. Then answer the following questions. Most importantly, think of your reasons for believing as you do.

- What were the possible causes for the spill?

    State the causes of each one. What do you think is the most important cause of major oil spills? Why is that most important?

    - Thinking of all you've learned, write a general statement by completing the following sentence, "The best way to prevent oil spills is . . . ."

        Explain why you believe your statement is true.

17 FIND OUT ABOUT

Some careers related to marine biology.

- Which is most suited to you?

- Why do you believe as you do?

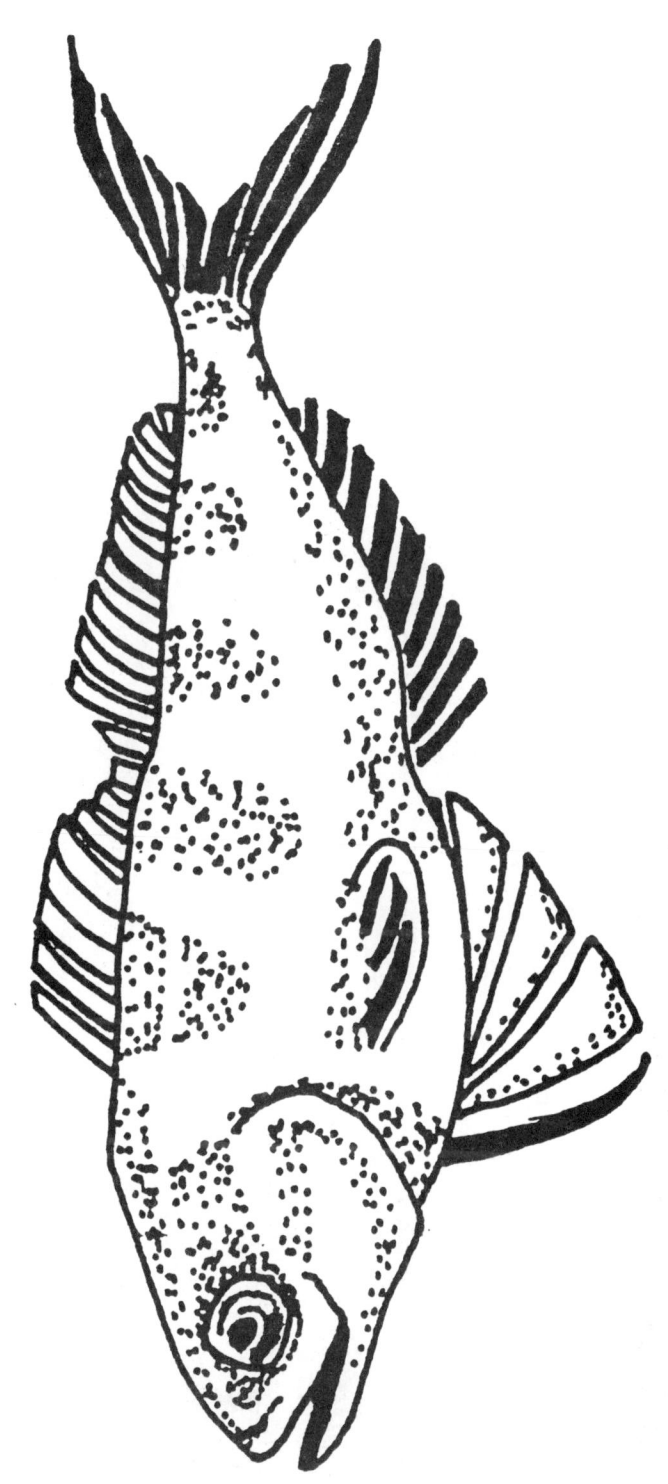

18 ART . . . CRAFTS . . . BUILDING (Choose at least one)

FIND OUT why the manatee would be welcomed in Florida. Make a poster or banner welcoming the manatee . . . be sure it indicates the reason!

FIND OUT about the coelacanth. Create a replica and write about its history. Display your work.

PREPARE a sheet of drawing paper "scratch art". (Using any crayon except black, color the paper solid. Then color over with black.) Scratch an underwater scene of:

- plankton
- jellyfish
- mollusks
- sea urchins
- starfish
- tropical fish
- sea weed
- any combination of any of these

Enjoy the painting "Fish Magic" by Paul Klee, if you choose this one.

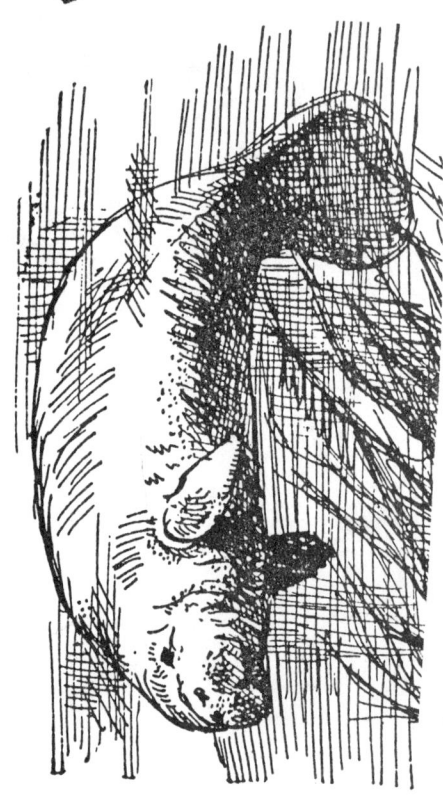

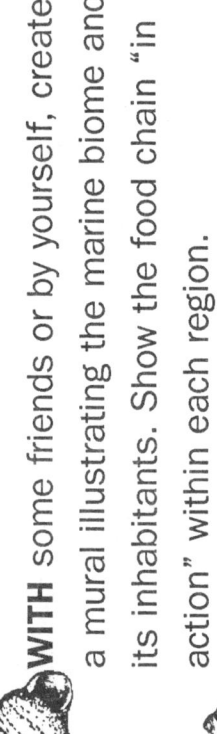

WITH some friends or by yourself, create a mural illustrating the marine biome and its inhabitants. Show the food chain "in action" within each region.

WRITE a puppet show about underwater life. Make the puppets and present the show . . . mermaids, a magic fish, a treasure . . . what will it be?

IN any medium you choose . . . water color, collage, wax paper and melted crayon . . . show the mood of the underwater sea.

MARINE BIOLOGY II ©1991 Zephyr Press, Tucson, AZ

19 LOOKING TOWARDS THE FUTURE

React to the statement made 100 years ago by Thomas Henry Huxley, English biologist:

"I believe probably all the great fisheries are inexhaustible; that is to say that nothing we do affects the numbers of fish."

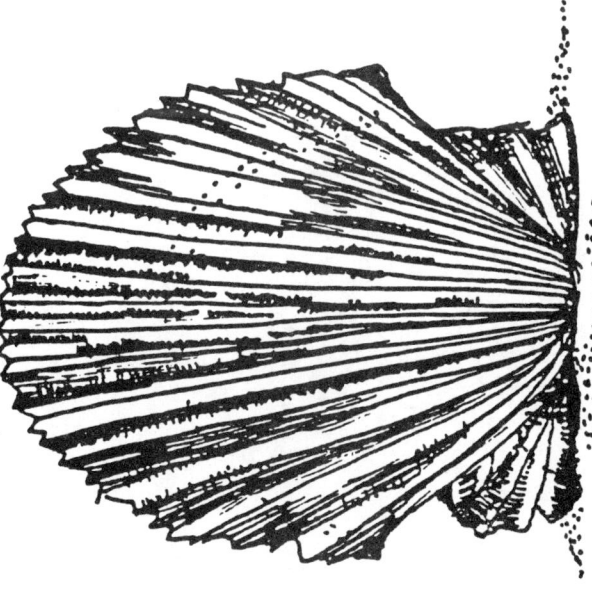

RESEARCH to find at least eight changes on the planet that prove this to be wrong . . . including technological advances, fishing methods and others. Evaluate these changes and decide:

Which changes have made the greatest impact?
Which could be controlled . . . how?
What, if anything, should have been done differently?

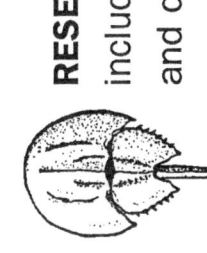

WRITE a news item presenting your feelings. Get it published if you can.

KEY
WORDS FROM THE SEA

BIBLIOGRAPHY

Juvenile

Arnold, Caroline. *A Walk on the Great Barrier Reef.* Minneapolis, Minn.: Carolrhoda Books, 1988. (Grades 2–5)

Asimov, Isaac. *How Did We Find Out About Life in the Deep Sea?* New York: Walker & Co., 1981. (Grades 4–7)

Center for Environmental Education Staff. *The Ocean Book: Aquarium and Seaside Activities and Ideas for All Ages.* New York: Wiley, 1989. (Grades 4–7)

Cook, David. *Environment.* From *Our Endangered Earth* series. New York: Crown, 1985. (Grades 3–7)

Craig, Janet. *What's Under the Ocean.* Mahwah, N.J.: Troll Associates, 1982. (Grades K–2)

Feeney, Stephanie, and Ann Fielding. *Sand to Sea: Marine Life of Hawaii.* Honolulu, Hawaii: University of Hawaii Press, 1989.

Grace, Theresa. *A Picture Book of Underwater Life.* Mahwah, N.J.: Troll Associates, 1989. (Grades 1–4)

Jaspersohn, William. *A Day in the Life of a Marine Biologist.* Boston, Mass.: Little, Brown, 1982. (Grades 5 and up)

Life in the Water. From *A Child's First Library of Learning* series. Alexandria, Va.: Time-Life, 1989. (Grades preschool–3)

Morris, Dean. *Underwater Life.* rev. ed. Milwaukee, Wis.: Raintree, 1987. (Grade 3)

Niesen, Thomas M. *The Marine Biology Coloring Book.* New York: Harper-Row, 1982.

Parker, Steve. *Seashore.* New York: Alfred A. Knopf, 1989. (Grades 5 and up)

Selberg, Ingrid. *Secrets of the Deep.* New York: Doubleday, 1990. (Grades 1–5)

Seymour, Peter. *What Lives in the Sea.* New York: Macmillan, 1985. (Grades 2–5)

Sibbald, Jean. *Sea Creatures on the Move.* Minneapolis, Minn.: Dillon Press, 1989. (Grades 4 and up)

Thompson, Brenda, and Cynthia Overbeck. *Under the Sea.* Minneapolis, Minn.: Lerner, 1977. (Grades K–3)

Updegraff, Imelda and Robert. *Seas and Oceans.* Mankato, Minn.: Creative Ed., 1981. (Grades 4 and up)

Waldrop, Victor, ed. *Amazing Creatures of the Sea.* Vienna, Va.: National Wildlife Federation, 1987. (Grades 1-6)

Wildsmith, Brian. *The Fishes.* New York: F. Watts, 1968. (picture book)

Williams, Brian. *Under the Sea.* New York: Random House, 1989. (Grades 2–5)

Adult

Cousteau, Jacques Yves. *The Living Sea.* New York: Lyons & Burford, 1963.

———. *The Ocean World.* Volume 2 of the series. New York: Harry N. Abrams, 1972.

Crompton, John. *The Sea.* New York: Lyons & Burford, 1988.

Gotshall, Daniel W., and Lawrence L. Laurent. *Pacific Coast Subtidal Marine Invertebrates: Fish Watcher's Guide.* Los Angeles, Calif.: Western Marine Enterprises, 1979.

Greenberg, Idaz. *Reefcomber's Field Guide.* Miami, Fla.: Seahawk Press, 1986.

———. *Hawaiian Marine Invertebrates Field Guide.* Miami, Fla.: Seahawk Press, 1987.

Johannes, R. E. *Words of the Lagoon: Fishing and Marine Lore in the Palau District of Micronesia.* Berkeley, Calif.: Univerity of California Press, 1981.

MacRae-Campbell, Linda, Micki McKisson, and Bruce Campbell. *Our Only Earth Series: A Global Issues Curriculum.* Tucson, Ariz.: Zephyr Press, 1990.

Menard, H. William. *The Ocean of Truth.* Princeton, N.J.: Princeton University Press, 1986.

Minelli, Giuseppe. *Marine Life.* New York: Facts on File, 1987.

North, Wheeler. *Underwater California.* Berkeley, Calif.: University of California Press, 1987.

Seibold, E., and W. Berger. *The Sea Floor: An Introduction to Marine Biology.* New York: Springer-Verlag, 1982.

Snyderman, Marty. *California Marine Life.* Port Hueneme, Calif.: Marcor, 1988.

Fiction

Anderson, Hans Christian. *Little Mermaid.*

Giradoux, Jean. *Ondine.*

Hemingway, Ernest. *Old Man and the Sea.*

Melville, Herman. *Billy Budd* and *Moby Dick.*

Mishima, Yukio. *The Sounds of Waves.*

Verne, Jules. *Twenty Thousands Leagues under the Sea.*

See also Joseph Conrad, Eugene O'Neil, and James Fenimore Cooper.

EXPLORING THE ARTS

An opportunity to integrate art experiences within an academic content area.

By Stephanie Grassinger

While each component, the self-directed learning unit and Exploring the Arts, is a complete and valid learning experience in itself, together they provide a more comprehensive and lasting educational experience for the learner.

 **GO TO THE LIBRARY**

LOOK at pictures of marine animals. Look for the following elements of design in five of your favorite marine animals:

> color
> > line
> > > shape
> > > > texture

DISCUSS each animal you choose with a friend or two.

LIST your observations.

 **DO** a drawing with crayons or oil pastels of an underwater scene. Draw marine animals and plant life. Invent some living creatures of your own.

COLOR your drawing with heavy strokes. Use water color and paint for the water. Wash the watercolor paint over your entire drawing. The heavy crayon will resist the paint. The paint will stain the paper wherever you did not color. This is called crayon resist.

IMPORTANT
Wash your paint on lightly. Do not "scrub" it.

MAKE A SCULPTURE

INVENT AN ANIMAL
Let all of the research you have completed inspire you with an idea. Invent a marine animal. Make a sketch of your idea.

Use newspaper, cardboard, egg cartons, etc., to build your animal. Tape or string is good for holding sections together. The newspaper base is called an *armature*. Cover the *armature* with strips of newspaper dipped in papier-mâché. Give it two coats or layers. The papier-mâché will dry in a day or two. When the sculpture is dry, sand any rough spots you may have with a fine grade sandpaper. Now you are ready to paint. Paint your animal.

Zephyr Learning Packets

Humanities & Social Studies Series

You'll learn with *Zephyr Learning Packets* along with your students! That's what teachers say about this best-selling series. These interdisciplinary research-based packets are just what the teacher ordered to inspire every kid in the classroom!

Here are 25 jam-packed activity units that promote critical and creative thinking and provide students with hands-on problem-solving, research, and higher-level thinking skills. Students discover the excitement of self-directed study with these absorbing topics. The best part ... you facilitate the process and your students do the learning.

The Learning Packets —
- Are reproducible for each student
- Require student research and reporting
- Promote critical and creative thinking
- Need little teacher preparation or supervision
- Are easy to use

Each Packet Includes —
- Interdisciplinary and integrative activities
- Complete bibliography
- Art exploration section
- Learning center ideas
- Two units: K-3 & 4-8

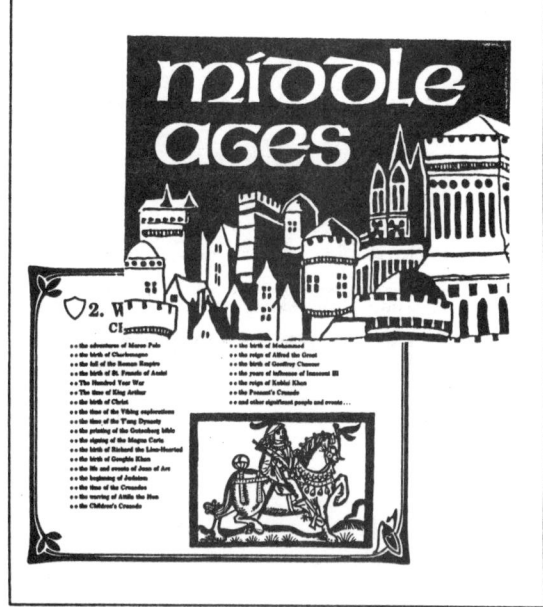

NEW!
The Blue and the Gray
America's Civil War (1861-1865)
by Carol Hauswald and Earl Bitoy (1992)
Your students will explore the causes and effects of the American Civil War, the war that forged our *United States*. This high-interest unit promotes independent discovery as well as learning-center/task-card activities for cooperative learning.
ZP20-W $19.95

Early People
by Beaham and Tanner (1983)
Students uncover the mysteries of early people and culture. They'll research the discovery of fire, the development of tools, weapons, and agriculture in the context of the Pleistocene, Paleolithic, Mesolithic, and Neolithic periods.
ZP06-W $19.95

Wassily Kandinsky
by Stephany Grassinger (1980)
Kids love Kandinsky because his style is much fun to recreate. They'll share his love of color and shape as they explore the artist's perspective and his stylistic development.
ZM05-W $19.95

NEW!
Jade Garden
Ancient to Modern China
by Carol Hauswald and Earl Bitoy (1991)
Open the door to the study of Chinese culture with the innovative activities in this new *Zephyr Learning Packet*. With its romantic past and ever-changing present, the study of China has never been more timely.
ZP19-W $19.95

Middle Ages
by Joey Tanner (1981)
Crusade through time as students investigate the Dark Ages and create a time line through the birth of Christ through the reign of Kublai Khan.
ZP07-W $19.95

Old Russia 1400-1917
by Dianne Jones (1989)
Step back in time, beginning with the Mir to Imperial Russia — the czars, the cossacks, the Bolshevik Revolution. Students research Tchaikovsky, the Bolshoi Ballet and Opera, and the Mongolian Invasions.
ZP17-W $19.95

The Renaissance 1300 – 1600 A.D.
Man, The Measure of All Things
by Jennifer Moreland (1988)
Students connect the past and present as they venture into this inspirational era. And they'll learn about such fascinating people as Leonardo da Vinci, Johann Gutenberg, and Martin Luther.
ZP08-W $19.95

American History
by Gaeel Beaham (1983)
Climb aboard the wagon train west with this inquiry into the concepts and ideas that built America.
ZM01-W $19.95

The Americas
by Gaeel Beaham
A look at the Americas' pre-history — the development of agricultural societies, the purpose of a family, and the migration of early people. Students probe early cultures of Alaskan Eskimos, Mayans, and Incas and then present their findings in time lines, dioramas, creative writing, and more.
ZP01-W $19.95

Ancient Civilizations
by Clements, Domin, and Tanner (1983)
Send your students back in a time machine to the ancient Middle Eastern civilizations. They'll research economic and educational systems, including the alphabet, mathematics, and applied sciences.
ZP02-W $19.95

Early Japan
by Ruth Patzman (1983)
Say "sayonara" to boring research! Students take a look at the fascinating rituals of Japanese history.
ZP05-W $19.95

Ancient Greece and Rome
by Clements, Domin, and Tanner (1983)
The development of art and science in this noble empire created the cultural and intellectual center of its time.
ZP04-W $19.95

Ancient Egypt
by Clements, Domin, and Tanner (1983)
Your students discover the majesty of the Pharoahs, pyramids, hieroglyphics, the arts, and more.
ZP03-W $19.95

The Industrial Revolution of the Nineteenth Century
by Jennifer Moreland (1990)
Your students will explore this significant era in world history. They will study the social events and the technological and medical wonders that have changed the way we live.
ZP18-W $19.95

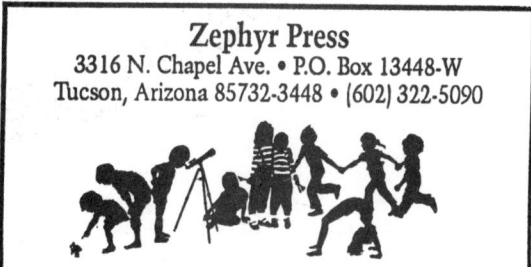

Zephyr Press
3316 N. Chapel Ave. • P.O. Box 13448-W
Tucson, Arizona 85732-3448 • (602) 322-5090

See Zephyr Learning Packets – Science Series for Special Quantity Discounts Offer on all Zephyr Learning Packets →

Zephyr Learning Packets
Science Series

These self-directed study units are flexible. You can select one subject for the entire class — or offer several closely related topics like Paleontology, Archaeology, and the Americas and students can choose their favorite. Copy the selected unit and conference with each student and let the research begin! Within the structure of each unit, students are given opportunities to —

- Make choices
- Learn at their own pace
- Learn in a manner more closely suited to their own learning styles
- Expand research skills
- Use a variety of modalities
- Plan their own time
- Develop creative and critical thinking skills
- Experience whole-brain learning

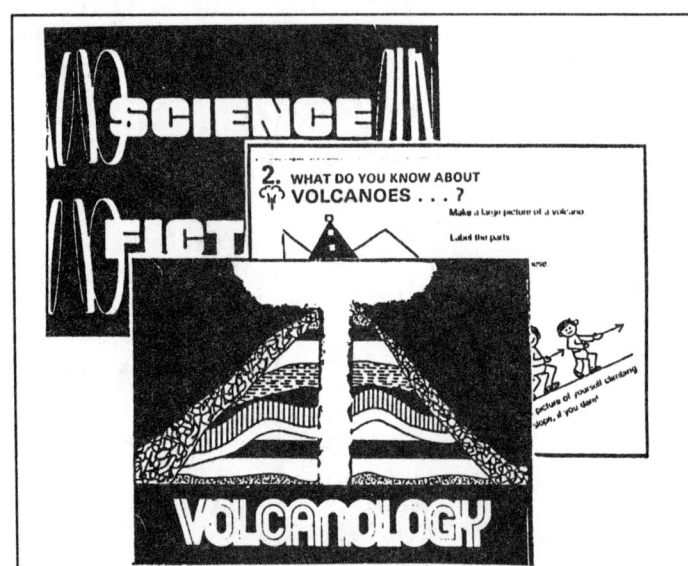

Futuristics
by Joey Tanner (revised 1992)
Your students will analyze trends, make predictions, and plan creatively to provide direction for our future. A favorite of forward-thinking educators.
ZM03-W $19.95

NEW!
Rocks and Minerals
The Earth's Natural Wonders
by Carol Hauswald (1992)
Rock hounds unite! Explore the wonders of those materials that are the earth's building blocks. Take your students' understanding of rocks even further by integrating this unit with *Volcanology* and *Paleontology*.
ZP21-W $19.95

Volcanology
by Bonnie Rasmussen (1983)
An eruption of learning — the facts as well as the legends and myths surrounding volcanoes.
ZP16-W $19.95

Paleontology
by Joey Tanner (1983)
Kids of all ages love dinosaurs! Catch the craze with this instantly interesting unit as they unearth extinct plants and animals, piecing together parts of a puzzle missing for millions of years.
ZP15-W $19.95

Ecology
Learning to Love Our Planet
by Susan Diffenderfer (1984)
Our planet's future depends on our children. This unit helps develop and expand their awareness of what people can do to create a healthier world.
ZP11-W $19.95

Entomology
by Clements, Domin, and Tanner (1983)
Eeeuooo! Students buzz with knowledge as they classify, collect, observe, and identify some of the 900,000 species of the insect kingdom.
ZP12-W $19.95

Science Fiction
by Patricia Payson (1980)
Imaginations run wild with this delightful literature unit. Students take a peek at cloning, robotics, body freezing, and other cosmic possibilities.
ZM04-W $19.95

Marine Biology
by Joey Tanner (revised 1992)
Dive into the ecology of the sea. Students study the delicate relationships between the organisms that make up food chains and the mysteries of the ocean floor.
ZP14-W $19.95

Astronomy
by Carolyn Zolg (1981)
This galactic unit goes light years beyond the typical look at the planets and galaxies with projects like building a telescope or sundial, designing a model of the solar system, and creating a constellation show.
ZP10-W $19.95

Archaeology
by Joey Tanner (1981)
Students uncover geologic history, artifacts, and finds as they research "found" cultures, compare and contrast religions of ancient civilizations, and create a mural of Atlantis.
ZP09-W $19.95

Geology
Our Changing Earth
by Diffenderfer, Zolg, and Tanner (1983)
Students unearth creative and critical thinking as they research plate tectonics, magnetic poles, potential energy sources from the ocean, groundwater and its pollution, controversies in river use, and careers in geology.
ZP13-W $19.95

Special Offer! *Quantity Discounts!*
Save when you order 5 or more *Zephyr Learning Packets* from these two pages! Just write in the individual catalog numbers of the *Learning Packets* you're interested in. Fill in the special quantity price from the chart below. Or go together with your friends to order a variety of topics — and save at the same time! You can save $100 when you order all 25 *Learning Packets*!

Qty.	Price/Unit	Savings/Unit
5-9	$17.95	$2.00
10-14	$17.45	$2.50
15-19	$16.95	$3.00
20-24	$16.45	$3.50
All 25	$15.95	$4.00

Zephyr Press
3316 N. Chapel Ave. • P.O. Box 13448-W
Tucson, Arizona 85732-3448 • (602) 322-5090

NOTES

NOTES

NOTES